BLACK WHITE SHA

Ina Jones

Illustrated by Dianne Ellis

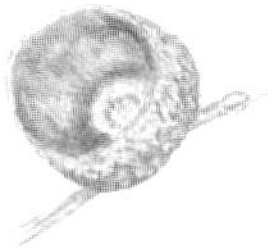

ARTHUR H. STOCKWELL LTD.
Elms Court Ilfracombe Devon
Established 1898

First published in Great Britain, 1998

British Library Cataloguing-in-Publication Data.
A catalogue record for this book is available from the British Library.

ERRATUM

Page 85, last line
for Can be honesty denied.
read Can be honestly denied.

Dedicated to the memory of my parents, with 'Love and Respect'.

ISBN 0 7223 3132-0

Printed in Great Britain by
Arthur H. Stockwell Ltd.
Elms Court Ilfracombe
Devon

Contents

At the end of the Day	5
Compromise	7
Perfection	9
Revenge	11
Cruelty	13
Determination	15
People	17
Pain	19
Caring	21
Love	23
Nature	25
Vicious	27
Jealousy	29
Trust	31
Memories	33
Temper	35
Protection	37
Weakness	39
Disappointment	41
Confidence	43
A Million and One	45
Time	47
Contempt	49
Acceptance	51
Kindness	53
Death	55
Middle Age	57
Adultery	59
Peace	61
Happiness	63
Survival	65
Worth	67
Commitment	69
Principles	71
Somebody — Nobody	73
Embarrassment	75
Hypocrites	77
Philosophy of Truth	79
Myself	81
Loyalty	83
Devious	85
Who you are	87
Progress	89
Violence	91
Compassion	93
Judge — Condemn	95
Passion	97
Humiliation	99
Honesty	101
Ignorance	103
Obsession	105
Loss	107
Despair	109
Laughter	111
Boastful	113
Ambition	115
Spite	117
Proud	119
Secret	121
Money	123
Friend	125
Joy	127
Contentment	129
Conflict	131
Marriage	133
Solitude	135
Despise	137
Weep	139
Criticism	141
Greed	143
Suffering	145
Grudge	147
Hatred	149
Fear	151
Faith, Hope, Charity	153
Sorrow	155
Gentle	157
Bravery	159

At the end of the Day

Dedicated to yesterday's people

The poem is my personal awareness of the plight of some of our elderly people who reside in homes other than their own. The footnote poem is a possible respite answer for the situation.

A sea of helpless faces
Saddened staring eyes
Bewildered, afraid, rejected,
An unbearable eternity
Trapped by infirmity
Reaching out
To those about
Pitifully grateful
For a helping hand
Having lost their own command
Wondering what will happen next
Trusting us to do our best
Praying to God to take them away
Not wanting to live another day
Feeling frustrated
Wanting to shout
"What the hell is this all about?"
"How did it happen?"
"And why to me?"
Please help me,
Please help me,
Is their plea!

You may love me
You may hate
But please do not ignore.

Compromise

Compromise
The perfect solution
To the world's ills
Also for one's own predicaments.
Compromise
Usually involves
Giving or doing something
We not want to give or do
But the end result
Produces harmony.

Perfection

To strive for perfection
Reveals the sad face of conceit.
To have perfection
Is to be truly blessed.

Revenge

Revenge
Reaps — relief
Then it
Reaps — repercussion.

Cruelty

Cruelty
Do not walk away
Protest to
Cruelty.

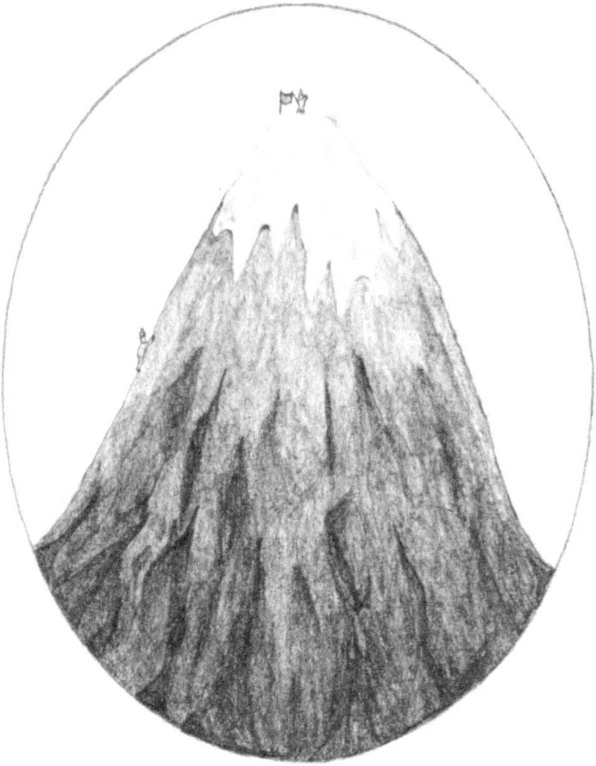

Determination

Determination rules the roost.

People

Accept
People for
Who and What they are
Not for
What you want them to be
For you yourself
May not be
What they want you to be.
We are all different
That is what makes us interesting
Tolerance of one another
Is not always easy
But necessary.

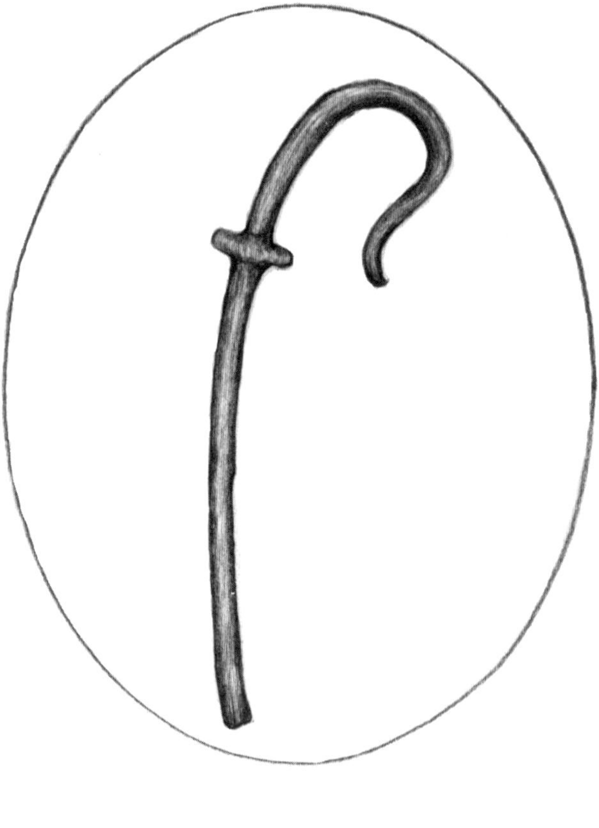

Pain

We all need help to endure pain
Be it
Mental
Or physical.
Do not be the inflictor of pain
Be the staff for pain.

Caring

Caring
Has two faces
Caring and doing
And caring and ignoring.

Love

Oh sweet love
Her weapons ever sharp
Her battlefields of broken dreams
Lie within our hearts.
Though love be not a perfect state
It is all we have to offer
So grasp her comfort, boundless strength
Go hand in hand with love.

Nature

How can the wondrous majestic
Sea be cruel?
She is only bowing to nature.
How can the wonderful magnificent
Wild animal be cruel?
He is only obeying nature.
How can the conscience-minded intelligent
Human Being be cruel?
It has been given feelings.

Vicious

Vicious
The Viper
The degrader
The demoralizer.
Do not take him on board
Have grace
And sail away.

Jealousy

Jealousy
Kills like cancer.
Envy
An understandable human emotion.

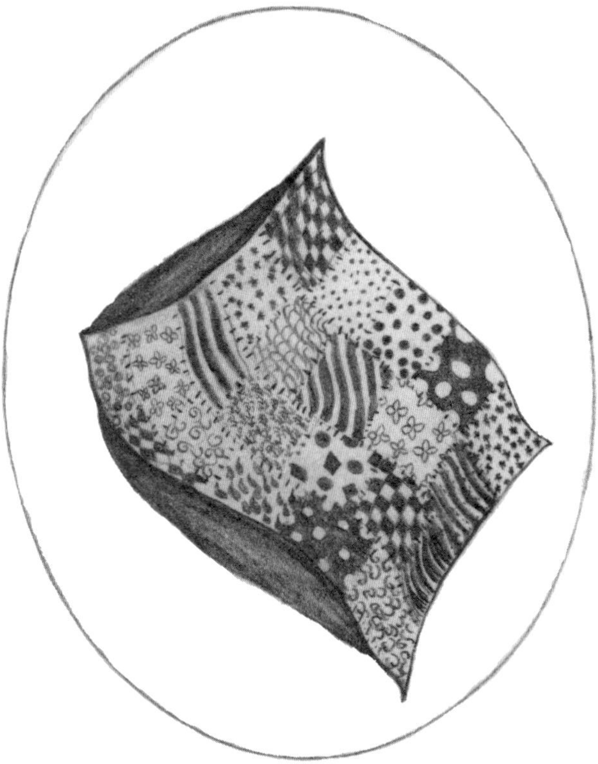

Trust

Trust
Patchwork quilt
Cosy and warm
Integral pattern
Has no form
Silent given
Immeasurable
Invincible
Qualites of
Trust.

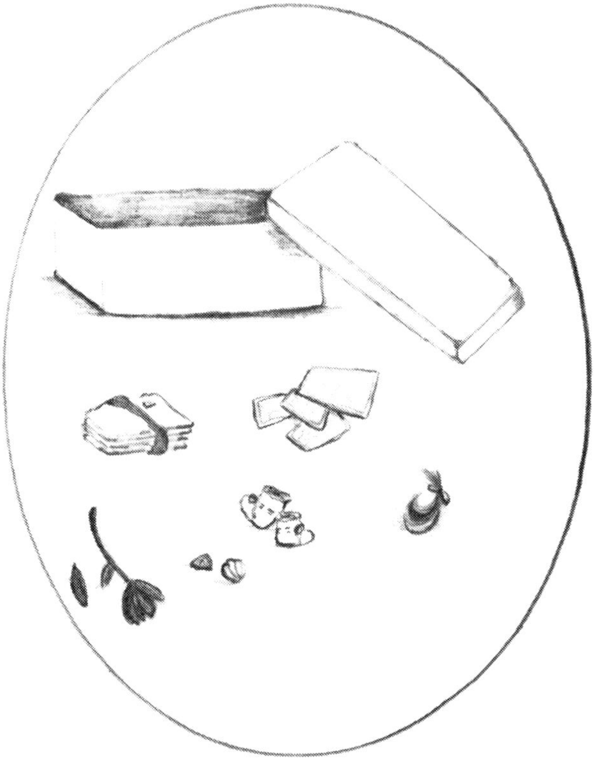

Memories

Memories
Vivid
Faded
Good
Bad
Intangible memories
They belong to you.

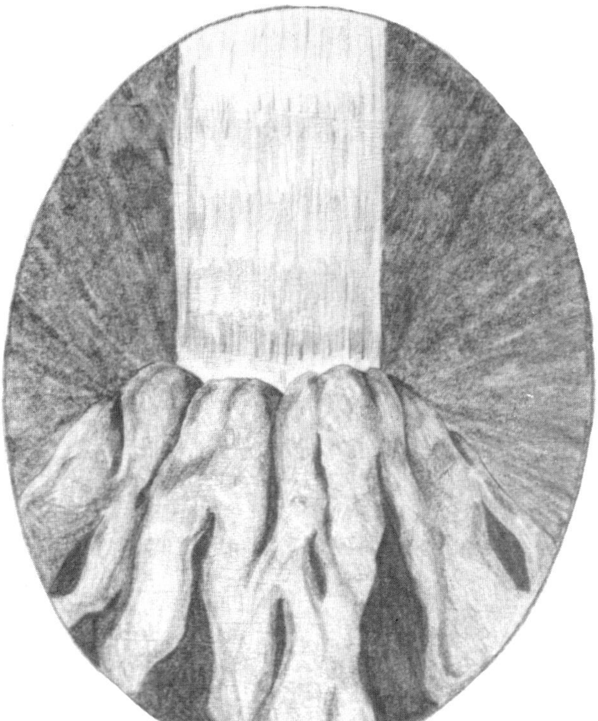

Temper

Temper
Your temper
This volcano in all of us
When erupted
Leaves lasting, sometimes
Irreparable damage.

KEEP
OUT

Protection

Protection
Such an inoffensive word
Yet can be so offensive.
Protection of
Oneself, one's property, one's child
Knows no boundaries
Knows no limits.
Plant, Animal or man
She will do what she can
The essence of our existence
Strong yet weak.
Protect Protection
Treat her with understanding and respect
Or press the self-destruct button.

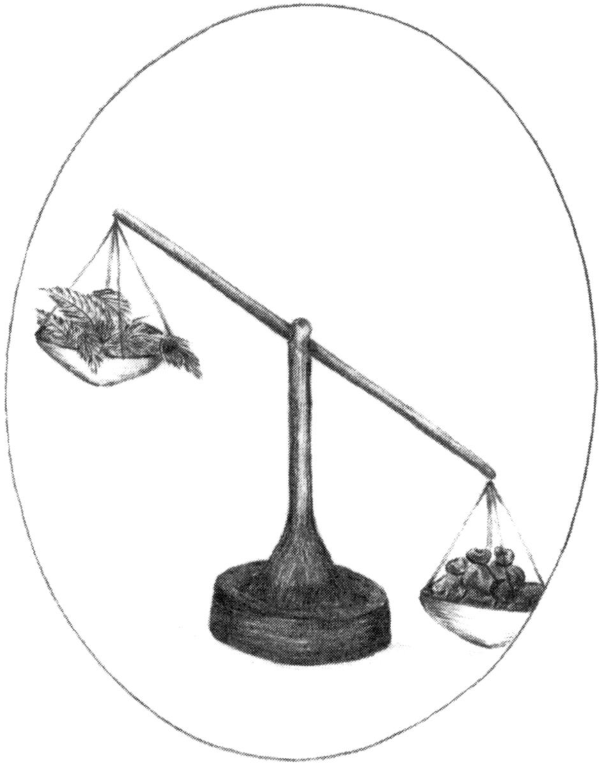

Weakness

Weakness
Should be pitied
It is the basis, necessity in life
Otherwise
How would we know strength.

Disappointment

Disappointment
Exciting — Expectation
Gone Wrong!!!

Confidence

Confidence — Thoughts
Another thing
I have not done.
Had I done
All the things
I have not done
I would have
DONE THEM WELL.

A Million and One

I look towards the sky at night
With wonderment and awe
And like a million others
Ask myself what is it all for?
The tiny shining stars
So meticulously placed
Upon the mat of black velvet space
So orderly
So calm
One cannot help feeling
Free from harm.

I look towards the sky at night
And feel her inner grace
Her secrets unfolding
Beckoning us to take our place.

I look towards the sky at night
With found significance
One can surely see
This tranquil beauty
Was meant to be.

I look towards the sky at night
With wonderment and awe
And like a million others
Ask myself what is it all for?

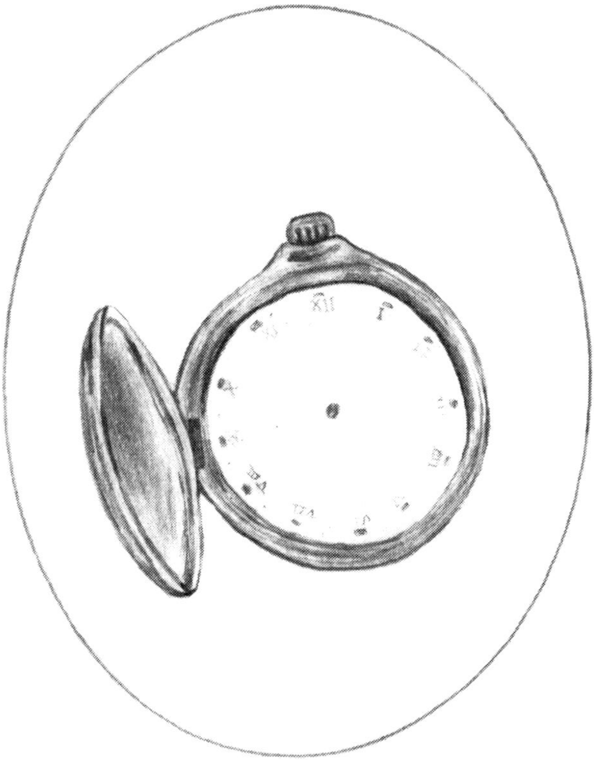

Time

Time is something waiting to happen
Yet has happened.
The complexities of time are endless.

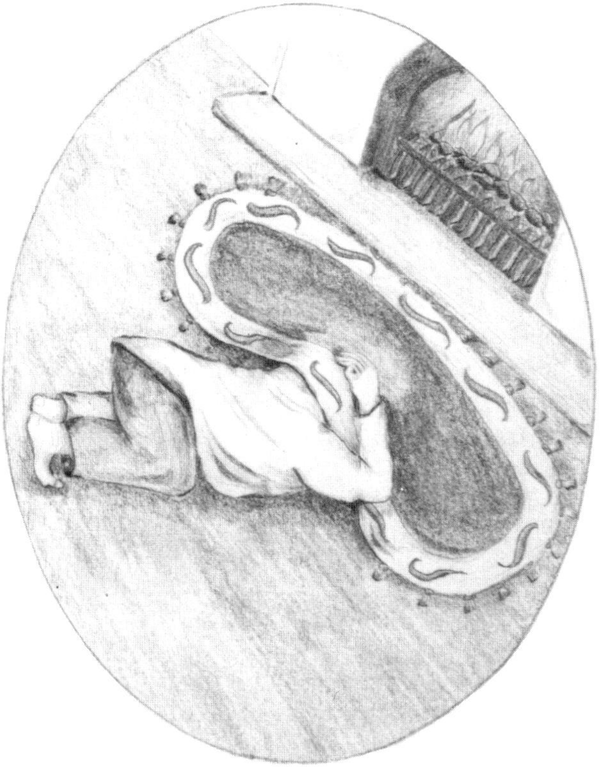

Contempt

Contempt
Contempt
She lives up to her name
Bringing strain and pain.
Treat her like a prison sentence
Do your time
The user of contempt
Liberal be.

Acceptance

Acceptance
Acceptance can be easy
Acceptance can be sad
Acceptance can drive a person mad.
Whatever her conditions
Whatever she dictates
Accept
Acceptance, she is a saving grace.

Kindness

Kindness never leave me
Always be my friend
Share with me your pleasures
For on you I depend.
Our world is ever changing
Not always for the best
So walk beside me kindness
And I will do the rest.

Death

Death
Is the inevitable penalty
For living.

Middle Age

Middle age
Dreams and aspirations
Fading into reality.

Adultery

Adultery
You are not breaking the Law
When you commit adultery
You are breaking someone's heart.

Peace

Peace
The extractor, the impossible, the possible
The perfect, the wonderful
The whatever, the whenever, the whoever
The something
We all need
From time to time.

Happiness

Happiness
Happens at different times
In different places
With different people.
How can one say
When one's happiest time occurred?
Do not measure happiness enjoy it.

Survival

Survival
The very root of our existence
She makes heroes of some
And cowards of others.
She blesses some
And puts others through hell.
The aim of survival
Is to survive
But do take heed
Not at the expense of others.

Worth

The position of man
Does not
Dictate
The worth of man.

Commitment

Commitment
Really tests
Never rests
So commanding
And demanding
Really reliant
Never sure
So afraid
And brave.

Principles

Principles
Are rocks on which we build our life
Having them can cause a lot of strife.
But what are we without them?
Just look around and see
And you will find the answer
To the question.

Somebody — Nobody

Somebody is Nobody
Nobody is Somebody.
The Reality is
Somebody — Nobody
Are Everybody
And are just People.

Embarrassment

Embarrassment
Is mostly of one's own doing.
Either way
Learn to live with it
Never try and put it right.

Hypocrites

Mother nature made us all
Hypocrites
Just some
To a lesser degree
Than others.

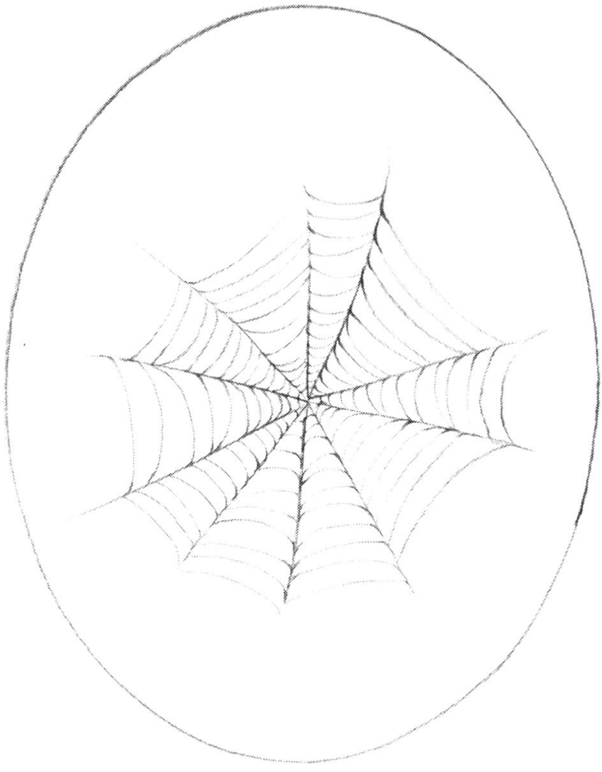

Lies can be dangerous
It is the truth that is the Bastard
But righteous.

Collins English Dictionary definition of Bastard "in respect, of the use of the word".

Informal:— Something extremely difficult or unpleasant.

Philosophy of Truth

The positive side of the truth, does not need defining, the negative side of the truth, if bared can be as dangerous as a lie, it can be harmful to one's person, and equally harmful to others.

Keeping your own council on matters relating to truth is not hypocritical, but essential, after all we are only human.

Myself

To be liked
It is essential to like yourself.

Loyalty

The fangs of loyalty.
A virtue?
A vice?

Devious

Devious
Of all the destroyers
The most cunning
Devious
Masks itself
And as a result
Can be honesty denied.

NO PARKING

Who you are

Never apologise for being who you are
Only apologise for being what you are.

Progress

Progress
The march of progress
Tramps over everybody.

Violence

Violence
Destructive
Self-destructive
Futile
Frightening.
Violence has no winners
Only sinners.

Compassion

Compassion
Lends a hand to humanity.

Judge — Condemn

Judge — Condemn
We are given the ability
To Judge
But not the right
To condemn.

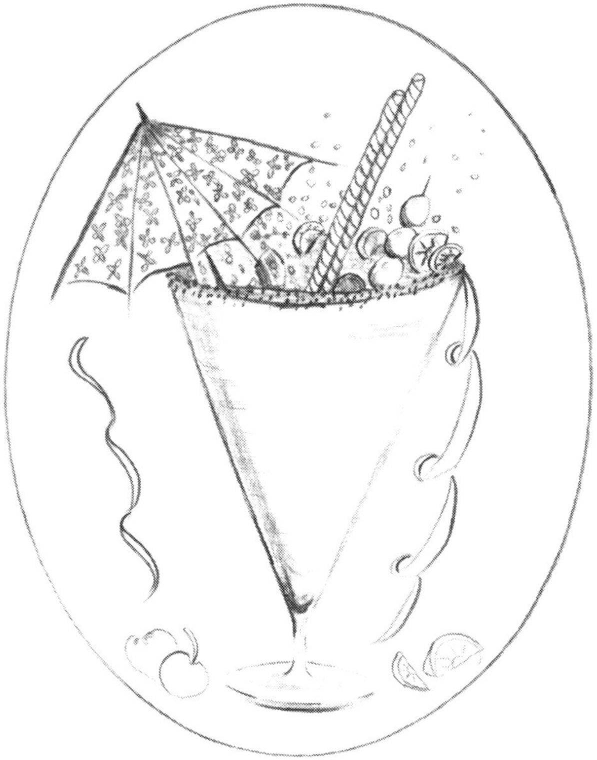

Passion

Passion people
All consuming
Blinkered senses
Danger is their name
Wanting, having, being, seeing
Excitement, pride, love
The needed extraordinary intoxicating cocktail
Called passion.

Humiliation

Humiliation, Humiliation
You do not work alone
You prey upon the innocent
And leave them, in despair
You give arms to the bad
To me you are so sad.

Honesty

Honesty
So freely given
Be careful not to hurt
Or to be hurt
For honesty
Can make and break.

Ignorance

Do not be afraid
To admit to ignorance
It is an excellent form of learning.

Obsession

Obsession
An uncontrollable
State of mind.

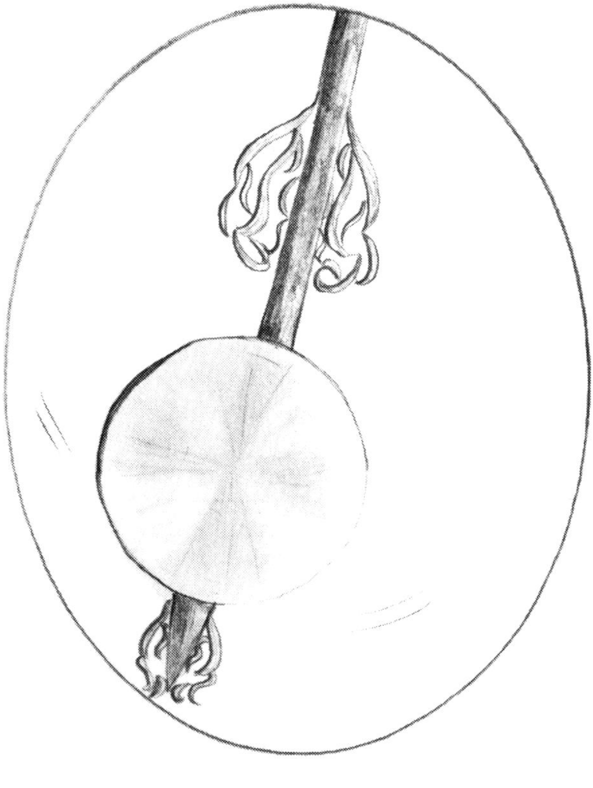

Loss

Loss
Whether it be
A person
A thing
Or
A feeling
Nearly always involves
Something you cannot replace.
Accepting loss is hard
But possible
People, things, and feelings
Do not last for ever
It is only time that does.

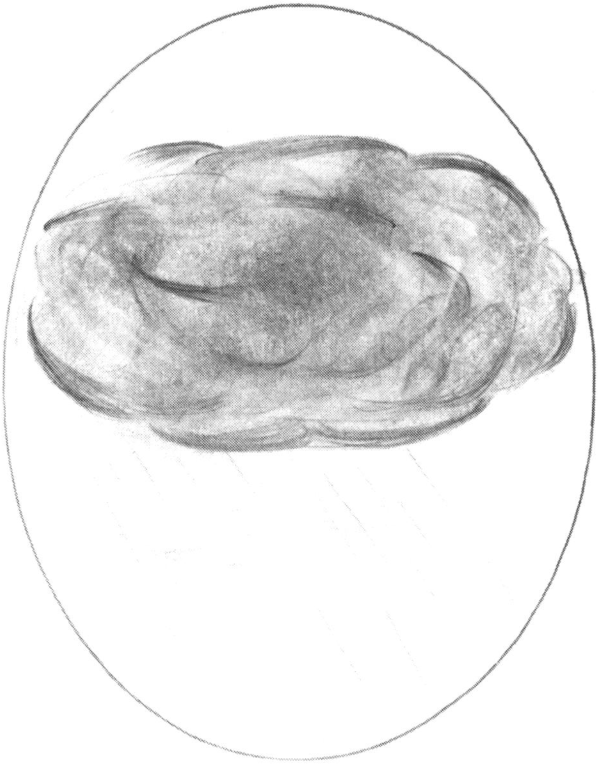

Despair

Despair
The taker of all your emotions.
Do not give to despair
Care about it.
Care about your own despair
Fight back take back
Do not let her keep your soul.

Laughter

Laughter
Soul Music
Babies' Chuckles
Teenage Giggles
Grandpa Roars
The melody of laughter
Totally free to all.

Boastful

Boastful
Sows the seeds of jealousy
Avoid him if you can.

Ambition

Ambition
Produces casualties
It also produces empires.

Spite

Spite
Stems from childhood
It rarely blossoms.

Proud

Be proud
To be proud
It is not a bad thing.

Secret

How we cope with a secret
Determines the very nature of our being.

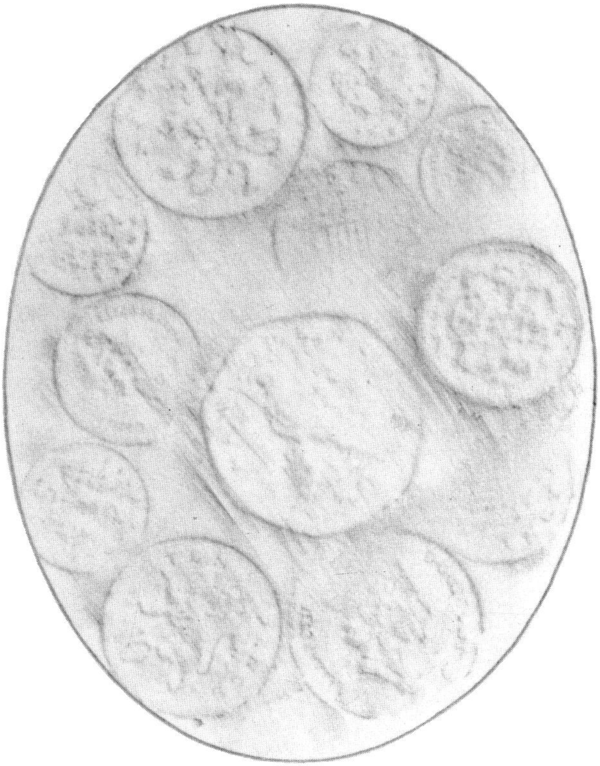

Money

Money
The universal communicator
Be it friend or foe
It knows no class.

Friend

Be your own best friend
It leaves
No room
For complaint.
On the other hand
A friend
At any level
Can act as an anchor
Securing and protecting.

Joy

Joy
The ultimate state of happiness.

Contentment

Contentment
The state of bliss,
Being, contentment
Contented with
Who you are
What you are
What you have
What you do not have
Welcome contentment
And open the door to freedom.

Conflict

Conflict
Bears more pain
Than we realize.
Conflict is a real problem
And should be listened to more carefully.

Marriage

You're starting out together
Upon life's bumpy road
And things won't always be
What you have been told.
There will be ups
There will be downs
There will be joys
There will be frowns.
You will be Mum
You will be Dad
You will feel glad
You will feel sad.
But what you must remember
Is what it's all about
Is loving one another throughout.

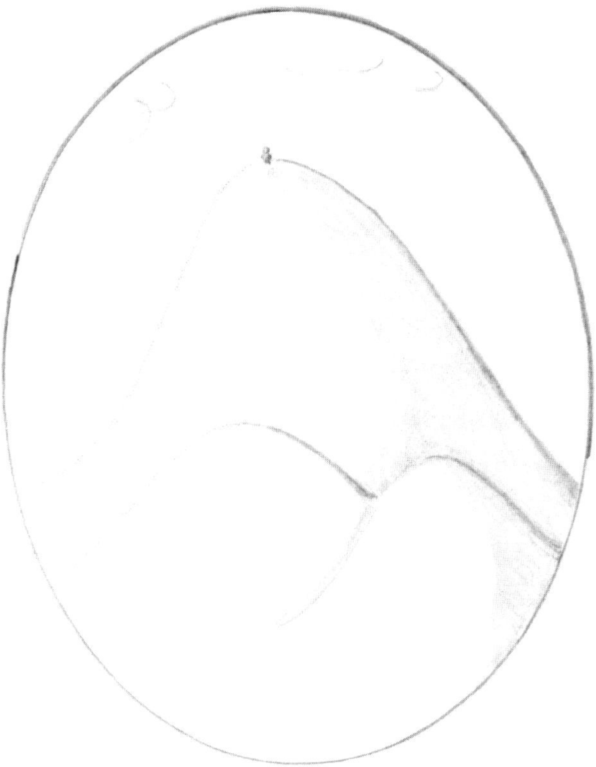

Solitude

Solitude
It has compensations
For a while.

Despise

Despise
Of oneself
And of others
Cuts deep into your heart.
It twists the double-edged blade
Of guilt and dislike
Hurting, hating, taking.
How do we help this plight?
The answer though be not easy
Lies within yourself.
Blame Shame
Accept Responsibility
Accept Reason
Accept Relief.

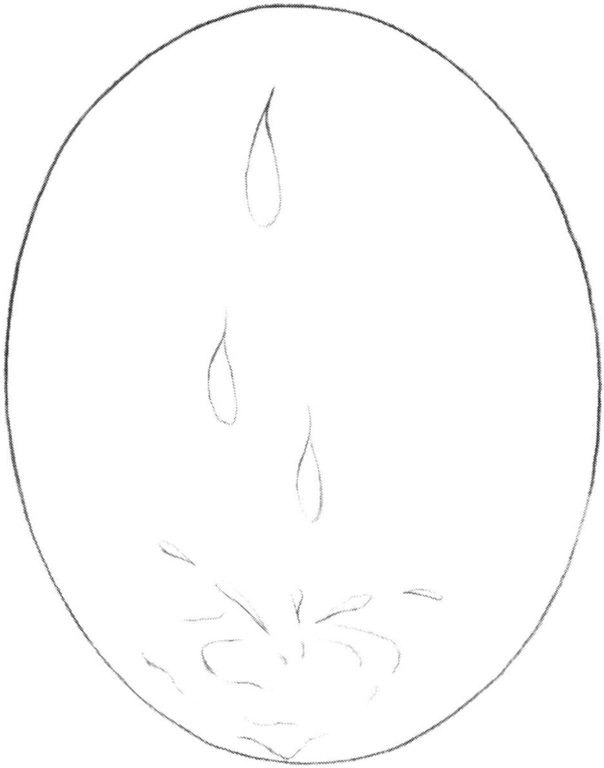

Weep

Weep
Then be happy
If you still hurt
Weep again.

Criticism

Criticism
Good old-fashioned criticism
The character maker.
Talking or giving criticism
In the correct manner
Forms mountains.

Greed

Greed
Wanting something
You do not really need.

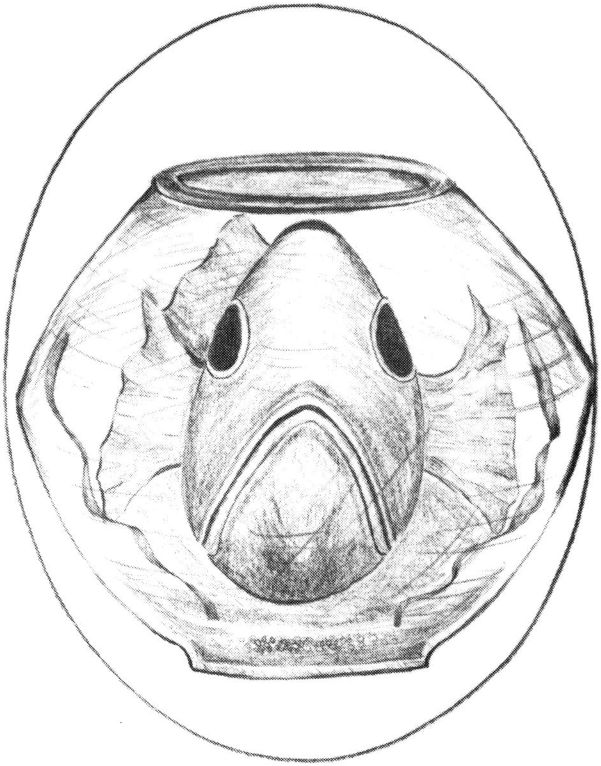

Suffering

Suffering
She favours no man
She favours no beast
Try and recognize suffering
And help put it right.

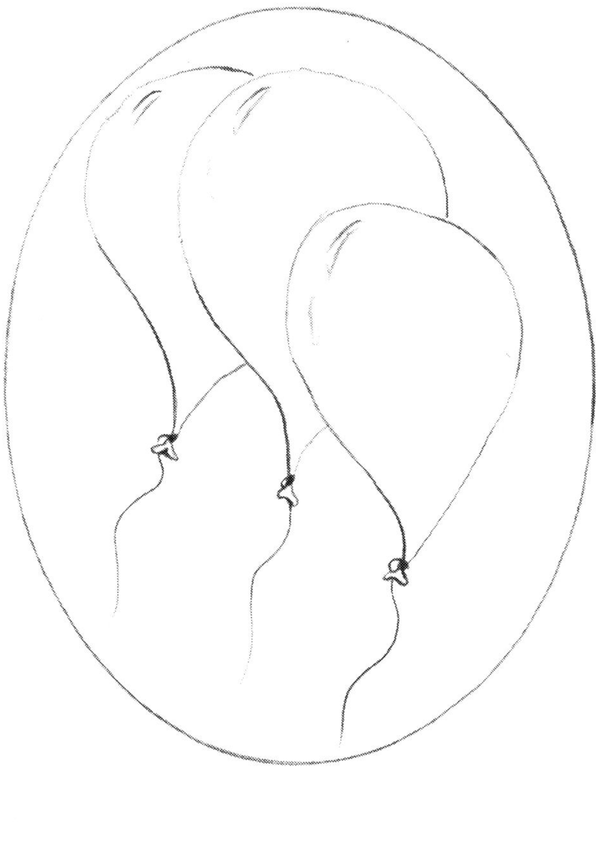

Grudge

A grudge
Do yourself
And all about you a favour
Try and let go.
Difficult though it may be
It is the only road to take
To gain peace of mind.

Hatred

Hatred
Ugly, understandable, unwanted
Bear it with dignity
And it will go away.

Fear

Fear has many forms
Too numerous to comprehend.

Faith, Hope, Charity

Faith, Hope, Charity
The three little sisters.
Have Faith in Hope
And you may not need Charity.

Sorrow

We see the wounds of sorrow
The sadness all about
We feel the wounds of sorrow
And cannot let it out.
They say that time's the healer
The comfort and the friend
Please time fleet past
And make this sorrow end.

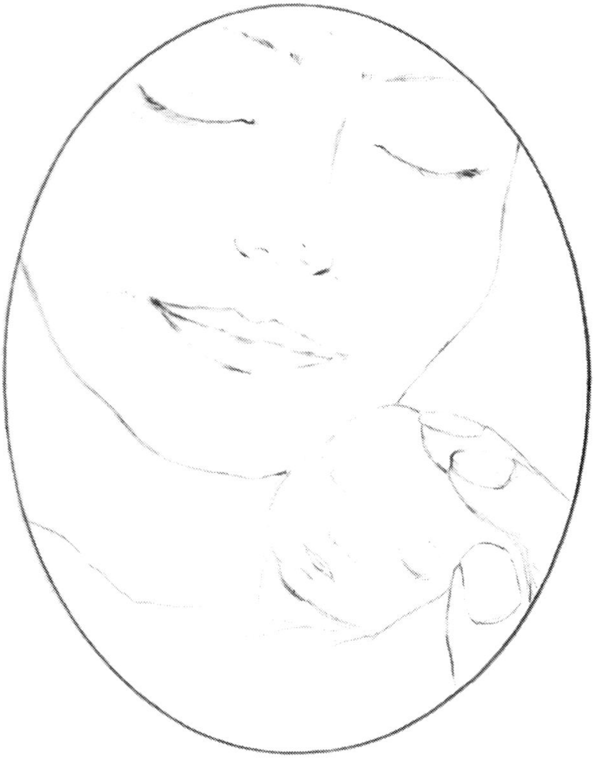

Gentle

Gentle
Wrap yourself in her arms
And be healed.

Bravery

Bravery
Is just living.